Cricket at the Manger

Edith Hope Fine

Pictures by
Winslow Pels

Boyds Mills Press

Boyds Mills Press, Inc.
A Highlights Company
815 Church Street
Honesdale, Pennsylvania 18431
Printed in China

Library of Congress Cataloging-in-Publication Data

Fine, Edith Hope.
  Cricket at the manger / by Edith Hope Fine ; illustrated by Winslow Pels.— 1st ed.
    p. cm.
  Summary: A cricket, grouchy about being awakened by strange noises, makes
his way to their source—a manger in which a baby waits to hear his song.
  ISBN 1-56397-993-4 (alk. paper)
  [1. Crickets—Fiction. 2. Jesus Christ—Nativity—Fiction. 3. Christmas—Fiction.]
I. Pels, Winslow, 1947- ill. II. Title.

  PZ7.F495674Cri 2005
  [E]—dc22

2004029070

First edition, 2005
The text of this book is set in 17-point Papyrus.
The illustrations are done in mixed medium.

Visit our Web site at www.boydsmillspress.com

10 9 8 7 6 5 4 3 2 1

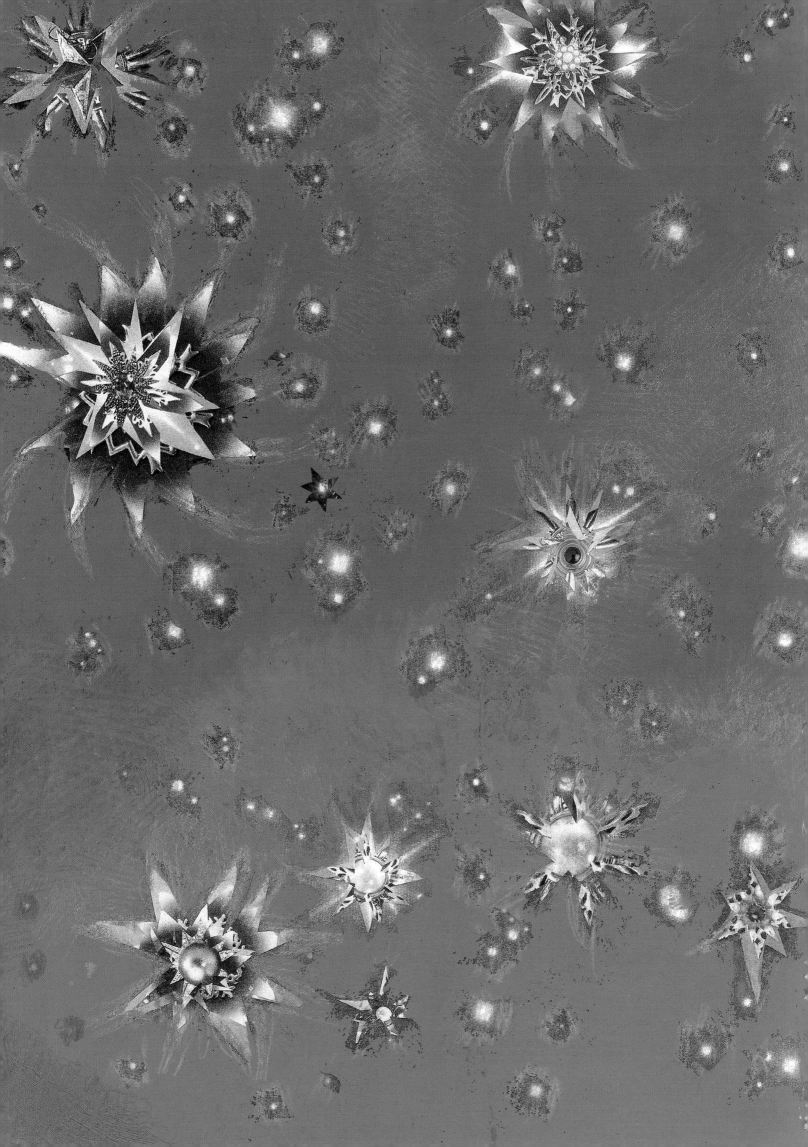

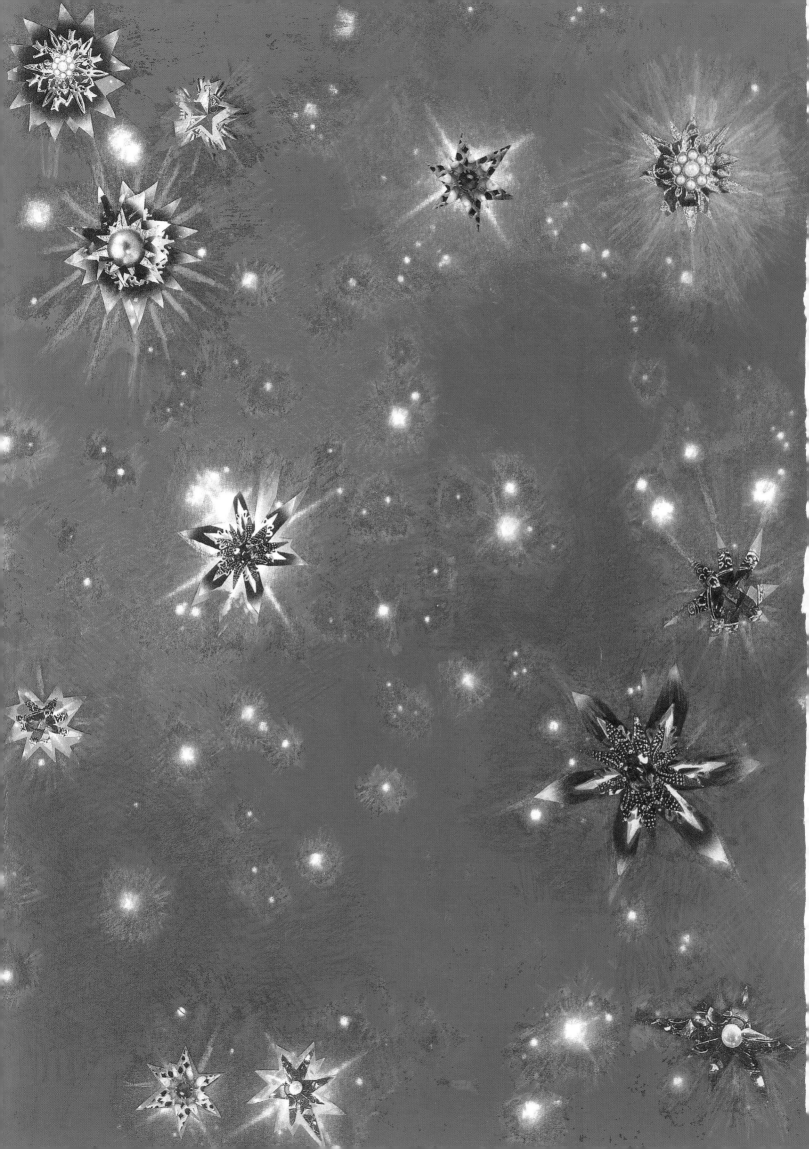

In loving memory of Gertrude Cameron Woodbridge Hope,
my remarkable mother—optimist, fey spirit, bibliophile.
— E. H. F.

For Aedan, little fiery one, bringer of joy
— W. P.

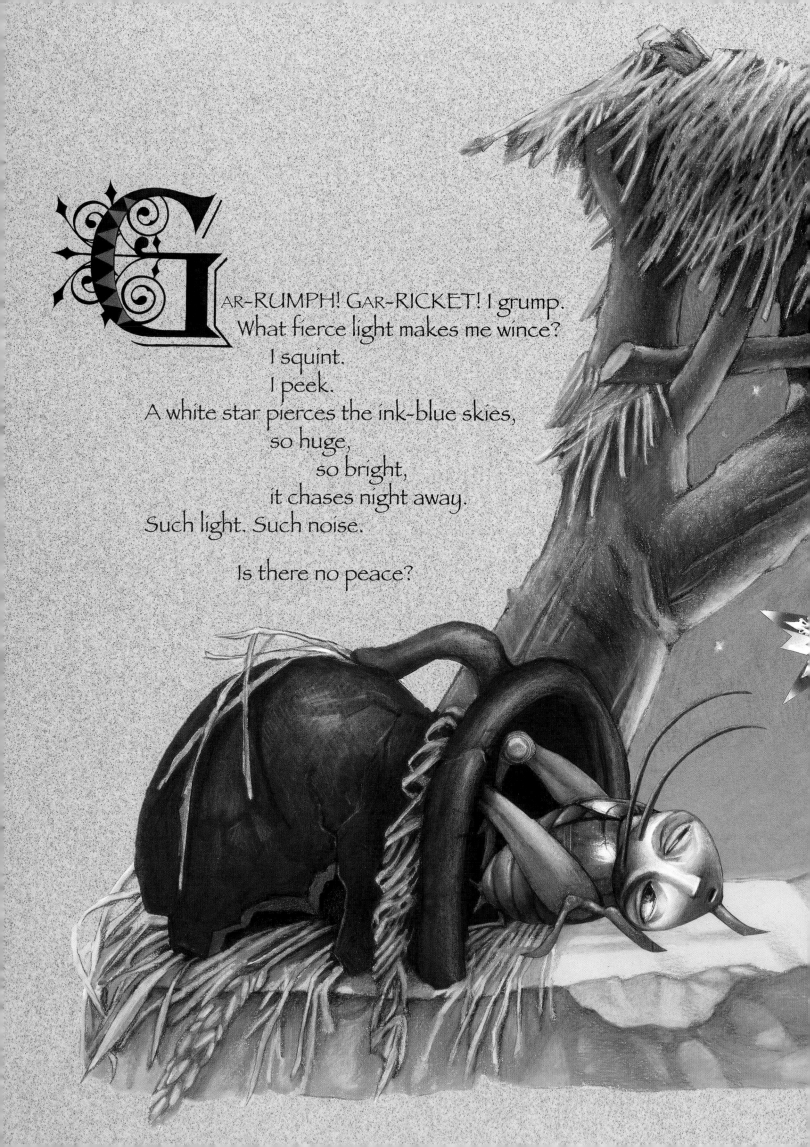

Gar-RUMPH! Gar-RICKET! I grump.
What fierce light makes me wince?
I squint.
I peek.
A white star pierces the ink-blue skies,
so huge,
so bright,
it chases night away.
Such light. Such noise.

Is there no peace?

The sun's long set,
 yet crowds still trudge the streets of
Bethlehem.

 What do they look for?
 What do they seek?
 A young girl's flock of sheep treads by,
 so close I see their woolly curls.
 Silence, you beasts!
 Can't a cricket get some rest?
Maybe I'm safe in this dark shed.
 I burrow under bits of straw to doze.
But what is this?

Cᴜ-ᴄʟᴜᴘ! Cᴜ-ᴄʟᴜᴘ!
More noise! More noise!
Cᴜ-CLUP! Cᴜ-CLUP!
Closer it comes.
In plods a donkey, heavy of foot.
A weary husband, with head bowed low,
leads his wife to a bed of straw.
He smoothes her hair.
"Sleep now," he says.
"Not yet," she says. "Not now. It's time."

Time! Time, I snort.
Gᴀʀ-RUMPH! Gᴀʀ-RICKET!
Time for quiet!
Time for sleep!
I drift.

Too soon, I wake.
    And what is this?
        I spring—click-hop—to see.

We're not alone.

Folk and beast have crowded in.
    Sounds scrabble in the stable air.
        A chatter. A chirp.
        A gabble. A grunt.
        Moo and hoot.
        Honk and squeal.
        Bleat and bark
            and jubilant bray.

Hush! Hush, all here!
Be gone, you beasts.
Be gone, you crowds.
Can't a cricket nap alone?

More folk bunch in, all humbly dressed.
I hear them speak.
"Glad news . . ."
"Bright star . . ."
"It drew me here . . ."
One totes a lamb—
It's the shepherd girl with her woolly sheep!
What brings her here?
GAR-RUMPH! GAR-REECH, I fret again.
No sleep tonight!
And danger's here.
I'm trapped in sandals and shifting hooves.
There's no escape.

Watch it, Old Cow! That's me underfoot!
	Stop it, Large Pig, or you'll squash me flat!
More people come.
	All telling their tales.
	Tongues trill the sound—
		"Thirrr-umm, Thirrr-umm!"
		"Strange sounds . . ."
		"I heard that, too. Thirrr-umm!"
What do they mean?
	I do not know.
		Such fuss.
		No peace.

GAR-REECH! GAR-RICKET! I scold.
They hear me not. Am I carved of stone?
They cluster now by the wooden stand,
the manger where four-legged creatures feed.
Each one, in turn, gazes in awe.
Each one, in turn, bows down or kneels.
You foolish folk. What do you do?
Have you never seen straw in a manger box?
And then . . .

Look out!

The shepherd girl!
    I freeze.
    Too late.
    She scoops me up.
    "Come, Cricket. See."
        Her nose is so close my feelers twitch.
GAR-REECH! I quaver.
No! Put me down!
She does not heed.
    She cups me in her small, warm hands.
        She lifts me high above the crowd.
    And now I'm riding through the throng—
        All hide and fur,
        All feather and fleece.

She holds me near,
 her fingers spread so I can see.
  I peer.
  I stare.
 What do I see in the manger bed?
  A tiny child in a halo of light.

Oh, listen now!
  Thirrr-umm!
  Thirrr-umm!

And what is this?

A filmy shape is floating here.
Its brilliant wings brush dusty rafters.
THIRRR–UMM!
What puzzlement.
I shake myself.
I blink.
Still there.
Still there.

The man and wife kneel side by side,
with awe and wonder in their eyes—
first at the creature wafting there,
and then at their dear one,
the newborn Child.
I watch.
I watch.
The mother strokes the Baby's head.
The father smoothes the strips of cloth
that swaddle Him, all safe and warm.

"Behold!" the shepherd girl whispers then. "Behold!"
I click-hop to the manger's edge,
landing just so, my feelers high.

The tiny Baby's eyes meet mine.
And then I know.
He needs a song.
I know.
I know.

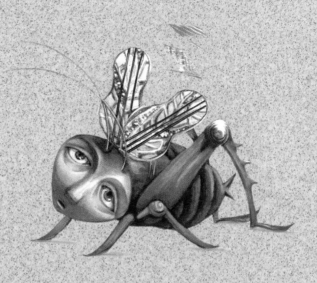

Wing to wing, I try to tune my violin, so long unused.
GARRR-REECH won't do.
He waits.
He waits, all patient and still.

But my tune's been GAR-REECH for so, so long.
Can I remember another song,
another way to play my wings?
How did it go?
How did it go?

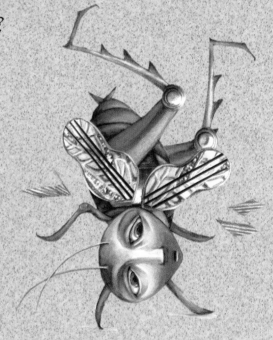

GUR-RIIIIP. GUR-RAAAP.
No, that's not it.
     I try again, with a scrape and a scratch.
  GUR-RUUUUP. CHUR-RIIIICK.
Wait.
There it is.
    CHIRRR-RUP. CHIRRR-RUP. CHIRRR-RICKET, I sing.
    CHIRRR-RUP. CHIRRR-RICKET, my echo rings.

I am only a cricket, but look at this.
The Baby's eyes are dark and warm.
His gentle smile seems just for me.
I'll play some more.
I will.
I will.
A chorus sings Moooo, Tu-whit, Tu-whoo,
to music of the thrumming wings,
and people's sweet, hushed murmurings . . .
I add my violin—Chirrr-RRRRUUUP!

Listen, you folk!

Behold, you beasts!
A Child is born.
CHIRRR-RUP. CHIRRR-RICKET!
All's well. All's well.
Sing joy!